LIFE - GUSTO - POESY

A STUDENT OF MEDICINE PLAYING WITH WORDS , WRITING ON LIFE

DR YASHENDRA SETHI

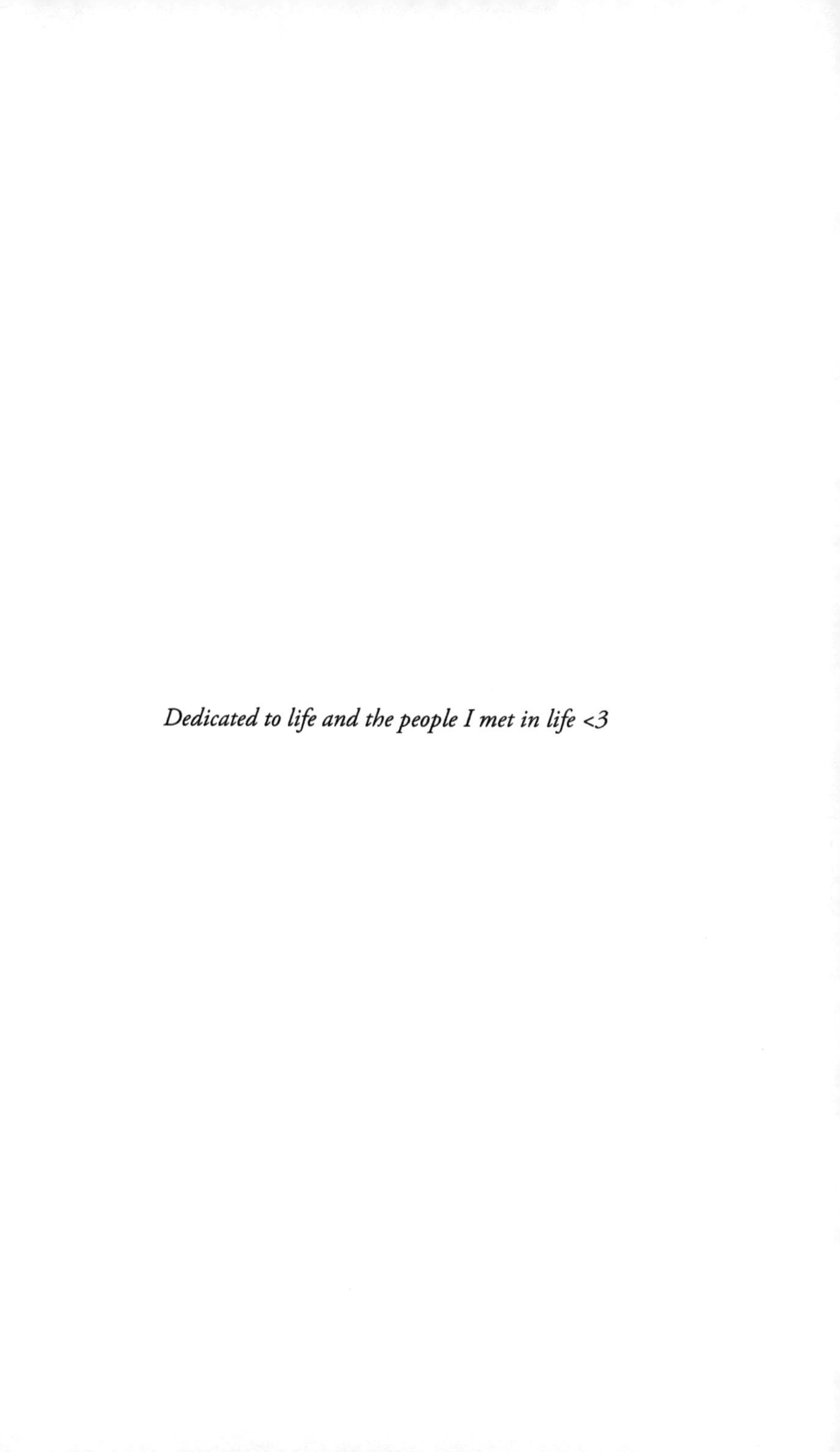

Dedicated to life and the people I met in life <3

Contents

Preface

An attempt to pen things you all may relate to,

As we all evolve through the journey of life, the experiences build us. We learn as we grow, some moments give us beautiful memories while some give us the needed lessons. Here is a little walk through my eccentric responses rhymed into words.

Promising you some quotes for insta story <3

Author name – Dr Yashendra Sethi

Social Media handles -

Instagram- yashendra_sethi

FB- fb.me/iamyashendrasethi

Twitter – Yashendra Sethi

Acknowledgements

I would like to express my thanks to my parents Dr. Narendra Kumar Sethi and Mrs. Indu Sethi , my brother Adv. Jayendra Sethi, my great teachers and my adorable friends for their support and motivation throughout my life.

I can not thank them enough for standing by my side, at all stages of the life and motivating me to trust myself for everything I do.

This publication is a product of the love I received in form of feedbacks from all people who read these on social media, related to them and motivated me to share them with a bigger audience.

Hoping that the readers will love the content and will write me back for feedbacks to improve before I attempt to follow with next version.

- Dr Yashendra Sethi

1. The Two Ways to Live

Way 1 -

Life ain't the way you think

It changes in a blink

To change your life, you have to accept

Control your feelings of regret! /?

It's all in your head

Because

Your attitude can be fed

You must learn to surrender ! /?

No solution unless you ponder

Find the easier escape ! /?

Say that sour were the grape(s)

You have to decide what you want

No one gets a prize to rant

Find an easy life and move on

Find sense thinking upon ? /!

The reality

Must create

Your attitude

Life ain't the way you think

It changes in a blink

Way 2 - *Now read bottom up* ↑

2. Ecbole

Maybe it was the first time
Someone seemed so mine
She also couldn't find words
Spoke her heart in a speech slurred
Probably words weren't a need
As the eyes could express the feed !

3. The Time will Come

The injured lion with every roar
Remembers the wounds that got sore
Thinking in disgust about the ones,
Who left him alone at the shore!
Life is like a game of chess
It's not just about with whom you mess
It's about how you adjust and respond
Time always offers both sides of the pond
Time is fair in being unfair to one and all
Everyone sees what is in their destiny's call
It's not in choice to deny the fate
But we can choose our response and its rate
Sometimes you need to pass a test
Before you can enjoy the best fest
Life will again be fun
The time will come!

4. Power

Something which is a wish of every being
To conquer and slay like a king
To establish valour, you start the sail
It's just differences that prevail
From those with power
There's sense of responsibility we expect
But when we reach there ourselves
The same do we forget
Often it seems like it's our fate to suffer
and wait for the knowledge we seek.
It's all his design, no one cuts in the line,
no one here likes a sneak
There's a balance in the way things are
Probably you will understand at the right hour
The problem probably ain't in the way things are
Maybe, your expectations are
***different from those in power** !*

5. Allow the Change?

As life opens the closed fist
And gives you the unexpected twist
You either go with the flow
Or tend to restrict and keep low
Opportunities knock only once
We need to pick our chance
Whether be dreams, life or be love
What matters is working for the right stuff
No matter what dream, things or person we choose
The life will offer a fight
You just need to find the ones worth enough
Making the journey bright
Trust the things and people that matter
The more time you waste
To say a yes
The lesser will you have together ??

6. Judging Others! Maybe You are Wrong !

Humans, the biggest brains
Got power to think and to train
It's not that everyone was created equal
But at least the ones stronger
Must take along their brothers who miss
Maybe life didn't give them the right kiss
Judging others is an easy job
Knowing the complete story is a must
Or else you will lose the trust
There is a reason, a person is the way one is
Maybe one didn't face things as he please
Do u think it's just the situations around that matter
People like us around play a role
But alas who pays the toll
So, let's take off our robe and wig
Let's accept our mates in their natural being
If you don't know the complete story
Still your judgment can be strong
But
Maybe you are wrong!

7. A Button to Rewind

A thought that triggers the mind
Wish we had a button to rewind
Looking at the glass of wine
Doctor thinks a stich in time saves nine
Days were those where happiness ruled
With friends you found so cool
Life then had just found the way
But then the twist, what to say!
You have an image of how things should be
But it's life, you can't ponder what could be
That solace and peace you try to find
Wish we had a button to rewind
It's the destination that matters not the mood
In search of a path, keep clicking re-route
Navigation allows re-route to find
Maybe life will give you a button to rewind.

8. The World of Power

You dream a world humane and just
Where truth and honesty are must
A world that accepts no lies
Offers everyone a chance without a bias
But ofcourse, dreams are different from truth
You must accept things, still do what you could
Power, they earned was just to rule
Expecting them to show responsiblity, you fool?
Maybe time will force you dead inside
And push you to go with the flow
You follow your conscience and don't bow
They will reap what they will sow!
But what can help, leave it on time
Allow the shade to pass and sun to rise
Keep smiling in dark waiting for light
It's just a moment, rule will again be mine
We have a culture of respecting others' rights
Cheers to a culture which just raised a fight
to protect self and not to invade
Allowing invaders to rule many decade
Its all power that we allowed to miss
Maybe Darwin was right claiming the fit

Ethics, culture, discipline may be your soul
But power that comes with time forms the core!

9. Anything is Possible

We live in a world that knows how to pull
And to decide a way, according to which behave you should
But cheers to the miracles that make it count
That make you believe, the supreme heard your sound
But the journey is special only if you can maintain
The nature and charm that you used to sustain
It's all about that lovely smile
That makes others feel that space is really mine
The fantasies and stories of unicorns and stars
Aren't to add to the truth
But way to make you hope, the way you should
The future looks full of uncertainty
But what's the fun finding something certain
The value of surprise is before the rise of the curtain
Things will surely find a way
And that moment you will call it your favorite day.

10. We learn as we grow but what are we learning?

As a kid we knew no difference
the world taught us to have a reference
Of caste, colour, status and sex
We would send a smile to a stranger
not thinking what the other person has to offer
We learn as we grow
we learn how to maintain those senseless egos
and how to make friends and foes
Loving others, inherent to humanity
Is masked by the greed of self-centrality
The mean world knows only one language
Money has been powered as the ultimate cure
Just think, isn't it making your life sour
You think you can buy anything
But dear, what about the cost
What about the selfishness ghost?
Growing up is a trap
A pure soul learns how to wrap
Itself in the foil of traits of greed
But days after satisfying your greed

You are complaining
The god isn't fulfilling your need
Humans the brains above all life
Think that they are civilized
But alas, we are no less than animals
Just that we know how to coverup
Our actions and traits of greed
Name it as "worldliness" And update our newsfeed
We learn as we grow
That humanity now called a trait of weak
Survival needs overpowering others
Humanity has become less important
than maintaining a winning streak
May be learning is a process to ponder
It maybe about destroying all fake ghosts
Growing over your fears learning from pure souls
No matter how polluted the sky is found
A rain is enough to settle it all down!

11. Shade

Flowers born to bloom
Adore the sun, not the moon
But alas, time has its own ways
Shade follows the mighty brightness of days
All that a human can do is to accept and respect the time
Knowing that the shade isn't permanent either and the
brightness will again be mine!

Printed by Libri Plureos GmbH in Hamburg, Germany

9 798887 175553